Politics In South Africa

"Through the eye of a student"

Richard M. Mbokodo

Politics in South Africa: "Recent stories: 2005-2013"

© 2013 Richard M. Mbokodo

ISBN-13: 978-1492932543

ISBN-10:149293254x

Published by:

"Making your dream come true"

Reg. No.: 2003/060246/23

Address: P. O. Box 3663,

W/ River, 1240

Cell: +27(0)83 699 6200

Email: mbokodoministries@yahoo.com

Cover design, typesetting & layout
by Mbokodo Publishers®. Set, 12
Garamond, 6pt

Table of Contents

Dedicated to all Political Science and Public Management undergraduates.

Part I: Power and Authority

1. Defining concepts

1.1 Power

Power is the ability to do something, to get things done in a particular way to achieve a specific goal and sometimes it can be against someone's will. Power is the "capacity to bring about intended effects" (Hague & Harrop 2010:10). Roger defines power as "the ability to achieve whatever effect is desired, whether or not in the face of opposition" (2007:543). For example, a person having the necessary experience and skill to drive a car has power to do that.

1.2 Authority

Authority can be defined as the right to use power. Authority is "that feature of a person, role, office or government which authorizes (i.e. makes legitimate, either in reality or in appearance) the acts and commands exercised in his or its name" (Roger 2007:47). For example, one can be assigned in a higher position and those under his command should listen and follow his orders.

Christopher (2013) gave examples where power and authority can be seen saying that "any person or entity may claim to have power in some regard, but they must have the authority to back that claim. A company or government car is right in front of a person, and the power to drive it is there, but they do not have the permission to drive the car"

2. Different types of authority as identified by Weber

"Weber developed a particularly influential concept of authority in distinguishing three ways of validating political power: by tradition, by charisma and by appeal to legal-rational norms" (Hague& Harrop 2010:12).

2.1 Traditional authority is when "immemorial tradition confers legitimacy" (Roger 2007:47). This type of authority deals with the rules or customs which are followed or practiced by a certain race or tribe. It instills respect for the elderly or rulers and "traditional rulers do not need to justify their position, rather, obedience is required as part of the natural order" (Hague & Harrop 2010:12).

2.2. Charismatic authority is the "intense commitment to the leader and his message" (Hague & Harrop 2010:12). It brings hope to its followers. This is an authority which is based on the belief and faith of their leaders. For example, Christians hold on to the promises of their Saviour which promises a better future as long as they obey and follow his teachings.

2.3. Legal-rational authority is where "acts are authorized by normative rules" (Roger 2007:47). There are rules, regulations to be followed and the office held by a particular official, for example, is respected, not actually obeying the person in it. "Here obedience is owed to rules rather than rulers" (Hague & Harrop 2010:12). It is important that those in office abide by the rules governing that particular office. There should be any maladministration.

I agree with Weber's classification of authority because they are needed to in order to have a "perfect" society.

3. Discussion about the differences between power and authority in the global arena

Power is often used to express an element of influence that could be utilised to achieve one's end. A clear manifestation of power in the global arena can be seen between the war that is going on between North Korea and South Korea. North Korea is threatening to use their nuclear weapons to invade South Korea. Scott (2013) says "North Korea is ready to resume talks with the

U.S and South Korea if they end joint military exercises and the United Nations drops sanctions" North Korea sees that both U.S and South Korea combined can convince the international community that they have to intervene to stop any nuclear war that is threatening the nations.

Another example will be that of the power and authority that the International Monetary Fund (IMF) has. There are 188 member countries and Christine (2013) highlighted that the International Monetary Fund has the power and authority to "foster International monetary cooperation, secure financial stability, facilitate international trade, promote high employment and sustain economic growth, and reduce poverty around the world."

Bibliography

Christine Legarde. 2013. Fiscal Policy, Equity and Long Term Growth in Developing Countries. Internet: http:/www.IMF.com. 21 April 2013

Christopher J. 2003. What is the difference between Power and Authority. Internet: http:/www.reference.com. Accessed: 16 April 2013

Hague, R & Harrop, M. 2010. Comparative Government & Politics: An Introduction. 8th edition. New York: Palgrave MacMillan

Roger Scruton. 2007. The Palgrave MacMillan: Dictionary of Political Thought. 3rd edition. New York: Palgrave MacMillan

Scott Neuman. 2013. North Korea: End U.N Sanctions, And Talks Can Resume. Internet: htt:/www.npr.org/.../north-korea-end-u-n-sanctions-and-talks-can-resume. 18 April 2013.

Accessed: 23 April 2013

Part II: Executive dominance is a threat to democracy in South Africa

1. Introduction

Most democratic states executive leaders (cabinet ministers and presidents) are in control of political power because they are responsible for implementing national legislation, formulating policies and coordinating the functions of government institutions. When the national executive holds much power, it threatens the democracy of the state.

This essay will focus on South Africa's executive dominance which is a threat to democracy. South Africa is a democratic country with a parliamentary system and the president is the head of government and also the head of state. The executive is drawn from legislature. This means that the party that dominate the legislature will also dominate the executive. A powerful executive is unlikely to be challenged by parliament and some officials abuse human rights to benefit themselves.

What is democracy? Democracy is "(1) the right to vote, (2), the right to be elected, (3) the right of political leaders to compete for support and votes, (4) elections that are free and fair, (5) freedom of association, (6) freedom of expression, (7) alternative sources of information, and (8) institutions for making public policies depends on voted and the expressions of preference" (Lijphart, 1999:48-49). An executive that commands more power is therefore a stumbling block to a bright democracy.

One of the contributing factors of executive dominance is cabinet durability. The term of office is 5 years but it also possible for a new cabinet to have members of the old cabinet. The longer they stay in power, the easier it becomes to manipulate or pass policies that favours the minority and ignores the majority and this leads to executive dominance, social failure, economic failure, environmental failure and political failure.

The executive members remain faithful to their party as opposed to the electorate and end up ignoring the will of the majority.

2. Executive authority in South Africa

Structure

There are three organs of the state, namely legislature, judicial and executive. But we will focus on the executive branch looking at its structure, functions and assessment of the executive authority. The national executive is made up of the president, Deputy President and ministers. Mr Jacob Zuma is the President of South Africa. He is the head of government and head of state.

President Jacob Zuma is the head of the Executive and President of our country and as a first citizen, he must uphold the Constitution. He appoints cabinet members and other two ministers can be appointed from outside the parliament, example: Mr Pravin Gorhan. And he is empowered by the Constitution to among other duties to award national honours, appoint diplomats and also to appoint commissions of enquiry like the Marikana commission of enquiry and the Arm's deal commission enquiry. The executive is responsible to parliament and can be removed by vote of no confidence.

Functions

The national executive is responsible for implementing legislation, implementing national policy and coordinating the functions of government.

Assessment

The good thing about the structure of the national executive is that it is stable, adaptable and effective. But with more power comes more responsibility and a powerful executive can easily undermine parliament and sometimes get away with corruption. Those who are closer to the president sometimes get elected and they have in one way or another return favour or protect him. Some ministers abuse their executive power to benefit themselves.

We are all equal before the law and we should be treated fairly without fear or favour and one should not be given first preference because is loyal to the executive or the party's constitution.

Recently 11 African National Congress (ANC) councillors were dismissed because they were found to be disloyal to the ANC's constitution which requires members to be fight corruption and have good corporate governance. We saw on the news that the state will not pay for legal fees of the legal team that represent the families in the Marikina Commission but at the same time state lawyers are being paid by the state. The Nelson Mandela Bay Municipality manager has resigned due to the interference of the mayor and the Speaker. These are some of the examples of what happens when one is not faithful to the ruling party and is not even on the side of the national executive.

The enemy of our democracy is executive dominance and it must be treated before it is too late. Take for example the Oupa Magashula's scandal. Mr Pravin Gordhan dealt promptly with this issue but he is not saying anything about the state expenditure in Nkandla. Is it because he is one of the ministers elected by the president and he wants to remain faithful to him and to the cabinet or maybe he has nothing to say.

3. Assessment of South Africa Executives

The executive has legitimate power to enforce decisions. This system is strong, adaptable and accountable to elected representatives. The challenge that our democracy faces today is that our leaders have too much power and have large legislative majority and this tends to make some to think there are above the law and can influence the decisions of other institutions.

Take for example the Arm's Deal saga, it "has attracted much attention, not only because it implicates President Jacob Zuma, but also because it defies the core objectives of Parliament and the Constitution it claims to uphold: "The Constitution sets a single, sovereign democratic state where governance is effected through Parliament, the Executive and the Judiciary". The Constitution is regarded as the Supreme law of the land, which "lays the foundation for a democratic and open society in which government is based on the will of the people and every citizen is equally protected by law" (Law Teacher, 2012:1).

Other examples can be drawn from what happened to Advocate Pikoli and also to the former Police Commissioner. Advocate Pikoli was dismissed from his duties and this "came as a result of him refusing to obey an order instructed by the Justice Minister and Executive, to cease an inquest into the alleged corruption fiasco, whereby Police Commissioner, Jackie Selebi found himself embroiled. The Executive has too much pressure over the Judiciary, and as according to Advocate Pikoli "…judiciary should be guarded against as it could ultimately lead to the erosion of the independence of the judiciary" (Law Teacher, 2012:2).

We cannot run away from executive dominance but there must be a balance of power between executive and legislative branches and we also need stable and faithful cabinet ministers and they should comply with the requirements of legislation. Thornhill (2012:93) gives a clear picture of the balancing of power and upholding the Constitution. He says "every political office bearer (the president, deputy president, ministers, provincial premiers, members of Provincial Executive Components) and every public official should, when carrying out official duties, remember that the legislature (parliament, provincial legislatures and municipal councils-all legislative institutions), operating in accordance with the Constitution (1996) has been granted authority over his, or sphere of work and that it will always have the final say in every matter (again if exercised in accordance with the dictates of the Constitution (1996)" .

4. One party dominance

South Africa has a Constition which guarantes credible democracy and after the 1994 democratic elections, South Africans started to enjoy a wonderful transformation of this country and had hope for a better future. But over the years, we have seen changes which are a result of one party dominance. Some of the changes are good and some are not good. A party that stays in power for a long period of time and fall prey of executive dominance tends to abuse power.

The African National Congress' dominance in South Africa especially holding more seats in parliament "has blatantly affected democratic consolidation. The (ANC's) political clout has impacted upon the South African Parliament in countless ways. Most significantly, the (ANC) is vehemently opposed to approving reforms to alter the current Proportional Representation electoral programme, as this system is directly how the (ANC) maintains its majority stronghold. In addition, this Proportional Representation system is blamed for the social disparities between Parliamentarians and the public. Parliamentary oversight has been weakened due to Parliamentarians pledging their loyalties to their party superiors as opposed to the electorate. The (ANC) superciliously asserts its majority domination to put forward out of favour legislation and makes vital parliamentary decisions despite protest from opposing parties. Parliament have been criticised for exercising ineffective oversight, its failure to confer with society regarding matters of national interest. Furthermore, MPs have endured much condemnation for failing to uphold proper etiquette" (Law Teacher, 2012: 1).

I think this is the right time for our leaders to wake up and maintain the democracy we all longed for and wish to enjoy and benefit from it because democracy is not for the elect few but it belongs to everyone who lives in this country.

5. Democracy under threat

There is dark cloud hanging upon our beautiful country and if we do not do something about it, we will never be free to enjoy our democracy let alone enjoying freedom of association and freedom of expression. Two bills have been passed by parliament and these bills are known as "Protection of State Information Bill and the Media Tribunal Bill" (Nagan, 2012:1).

When talking about these Bills, Nagan (2012:1) says: "In the legislation known as the Protection of State Information Bill, we have a legislative effort to punish whistle-blowers with severe sentences if they expose to the press the rampant corruption of individuals in government, in finance and in industry. This secrecy bill is major legislative effort to institutionalize and strengthen the commitment to corruptheid. An editor who exposes corruption runs the risk of conviction under the bill for terms that may range from 5 to 25 years. The crimes include receiving information that one knows (reasonably) will directly or indirectly benefit a foreign state. A 10-year sentence may be imposed for concealing a confidential new source. A 5-year sentence may be imposed for disclosing classified information. And a 5-year sentence may be imposed for the failure to report the possession of classified information. These bills together represent a monumental commitment to the repudiation of every principle of agreed upon good governance principles worldwide. They repudiate transparency, they mock responsibility, they drown accountability, and they demonize the rule of law."

Our leaders should take a stand and protect the Constitution and more importantly listen to the voice and concerns of the people who voted for them into power.

"Society and opposing parties should insist that (ANC) and the Executive lead our country efficiently, recognising the importance of accountability within government, which upholds democratic ideals of government transparency. After all, the essential aspect of Parliamentary democracy, which must be preserved, is for the parliamentary opposition to fearlessly and unremittingly call upon the President and Executive to account in the way they govern the country" (Law Teacher 2012:3).

Conclusion

To sum up this important topic, we can say that democracy can be maintained but "it must earn and maintain the trust of its citizens. In the context of a transition from anti-democratic and authoritarian government to democracy, this challenge is compounded by the need for new democratic structures to assert their accessibility, transparency and representative capacity in the face of citizens' lived memories and experiences of institutional impunity, opacity, and illegitimacy" (Law Teacher 2012: 3). Our Constitution clearly shows the separation of powers, balances and checks and this guideline must be maintained so that we can all enjoy the democracy we fought for. The exuctive should continue to make and implement policies, coordinate activities of the state and also initialte government action. The legislature must pass legislation and also keep watch on the executive. The judiciary should contiune to interprete and apply the law and uphold the Constitution. Executive dominance is a threat to democracy in South Africa but a state without executive dominance is a state with a bright future and will have a successful and stable democracry that gurantees the rights of its citizens.

Bibliography

Law Teacher. 2012. *Dominance of One Party in South African Politics*. [Online]. Law Teacher: United Kingdom. Available: > http://www.lawteacher.net. [Accessed 12 September 2013].

Lijphart, A. 1999. *Patterns of democracy: government forms and performance in thirty-six countries*. Yale University Press: London.

Thornhill, C. 2012. *South African Public Administration and Management*. 10th edition. Van Schaik Publishers: Pretoria.

Nagan, WP. 2012. *Constitutional Democracy under Threat: South Africa's Dark Side*. [Online]. Available: http://www. readersupportednews.org> *[Accessed 12 September 2013]*.

Part III: Constitution

Question: Before the 1994 democratic transition, was the Constitution of South Africa supreme or not?

Answer: Before the 1994 democratic transition, the *Constitution of South Africa* was not supreme

A constitution is a blue print for an organisation and it lays out the institutions of the government, relationship between government and its citizens and it also explains the powers of the institutions of the state. Before the 1994 democratic transition, South Africa had an interim Constitution and it was not supreme. "Political players agreed that the new South Africa should have a supreme and justifiable Constitution and should abandon the Westminster Constitutionalism that had informed South Africa's Constitutional development up to this point" (South African Constitution 2011:xiii).

Chris Thornhill says "the constitutional dispensation that kept the white people in power was terminated by the Interim Constitution of the Republic of South Africa (Act 200 of 1993), which came into effect on 27 April 1994" (2012:8)

Question: Is the President of the Republic of South Africa directly elected by the Electorate or voting citizens?

Answer: The President of the Republic of South Africa is not directly elected by the Electorate or voting citizens

The President is not elected by the electorate or voting citizens but he is elected by the "National Assembly" (Thornhill 2012:60). Usually the President is the leader of the party that wins the elections and gets majority sits in the National Assembly. Our current President is Jacob Zuma and he is the leader of the ruling party (ANC). Our Constitution clearly gives directions as to how the President should be elected; "At its first sitting after election, and whenever necessary to fill a vacancy, the National Assembly must elect a woman or a man from its members to be the President" (South Africa Constitution 2011:53).

Question: Can President Jacob Zuma disregard the Constitution and any court of law in the manner in which he takes his executive decisions and executes his functions?

Answer: President Jacob Zuma cannot disregard the Constitution and any court of law in the manner in which he takes his executive decisions and executes his functions

President Jacob Zuma cannot disregard the Constitution and any court of law in the manner in which he takes his executive decisions and executes his functions. As Head of State, he is required to be an example by upholding the Constitution. Some of his duties as the President are: To appoint ministers and judges and he "may confer honours, appoint and accredit ambassadors and other diplomatic officers and consular officers, pardon or reprieve offenders, and make such appointments as he may see fit under the powers conferred upon him by the law" (Thornhill 2012:61). There is no option that can give our President the right to disregard any court because courts "are independent and subject only to the Constitution and the law, which they must apply impartially and without fear, favour or prejudice. No person or organ of the state may interfere with the functions of the courts" (South Africa Constitution 2011:92).

Question: In terms of South Africa's *Constitution*, which system has South Africa adopted?
A unitary, federal or quasi federal system?

Answer: In terms of South Africa's Constitution, South Africa has adopted a quasi-federal system

South Africa has a unitary system but federal characteristics and this makes it to be neither unitary nor federal but quasi-federal. We have one central government but have divided its authority through provinces. Each province is linked to the national government but independent. But even though they are independent, parliament can "re-delimit the provinces and their functions as contained in Schedule 4 and 5 of the Constitution (1996)" (Thornhill 2012:28). Each province can come up with its own sets of policies but "the legislative authority of a province is vested in its provincial legislature (South Africa Constitution 2011:61).

Conclusion

I have proven beyond any doubt that before the 1994 democratic transition, the Constitution of South Africa was not supreme; the President of the Republic of South Africa is not directly elected by the electorate or voting citizens, President Jacob Zuma cannot disregard the Constitution and any court of law in the manner in which he takes his executive decisions and executes his functions and we have seen that In terms of South Africa's Constitution, South Africa has adopted a quasi-federal system.

Bibliography

Chris Thornhill. 2012. South African Public Administration and Management. 10th edition. South Africa: Van Schaik Publishers

Constitution of the Republic of South Africa. 2011. 12th edition. South Africa: Juta law & Co.LTD

Part IV: Is it constitutional?

Question: Is President Jacob Zuma a member of the National Assembly?

The answer is No

The honourable Jacob Zuma was a member of the National Assembly before he was elected the President of South Africa but after that he ceased to be a member of the Nationally Assembly. The Constitution says that a member is "anyone who is appointed, or is in the service of, the state and receives remuneration for that appointment or service, other than the President, Deputy President, Ministers and Deputy Ministers" (Constitution of South Africa, 2011:13, sub 1(a)). Some of the duties of the National Assembly as explained by Venter and Landsberg are to make "the laws that govern our lives" (2011:23. As the Head of state and Head of government, President

Jacob Zuma can attend meetings of the National Assembly but he cannot vote.

Question: Was the decision taken by the former President of the Republic of South Africa Thabo Mbeki in 2005 to dismiss or relieve his Deputy President, then Jacob Zuma from his executive responsibilities constitutional?

The answer is yes

The deputy president is appointed by the president and he can dismiss him. The role of the deputy president is to assist the president in his executive duties or functions of the government.

Question: Was the decision taken by the African National Congress to recall or remove Thabo Mbeki as the President of the Republic of South Africa in 2008 politically and constitutionally justified?

The answer is no

The decision was not constitutionally justified. It is only the National Assembly that can pass a motion of no confidence in the president if he has violated the Constitution, unable to perform his duties or there are serious misconducts. In 2008 the National Executive Committee "took the decision to recall Mbeki without even going to the parliament and this is because the president must be a disciplined and faithful member of the ANC" (Venter and Landsberg, 2011:51).

Question: South Africa is currently faced with service delivery protests including worker protests and of which some have turned violent. Are these protests constitutionally protected?

The answer is yes

The Bill of Rights says that "anyone has the right, peacefully and unarmed, to assemble, to

demonstrate, to picket and present petitions"
Constitution of South Africa, 2011:10). The
problem with some of these service delivery
protests is that they have turned to be violent and
this is not constitutionally protected.

Conclusion

I have proven beyond any doubt that before the
1994 democratic transition, the Constitution of
South Africa was not supreme; the President of
the Republic of South Africa is not directly
elected by the electorate or voting citizens,
President Jacob Zuma cannot disregard the
Constitution and any court of law in the manner
in which he takes his executive decisions and
executes his functions and we have seen that In
terms of South Africa's Constitution, South Africa
has adopted a quasi-federal system.

Bibliography

Chris, Thornhill. 2012. *South African Public Administration and Management.* 10th edition Van Schaik Publishers: Pretoria

Constitution of the Republic of South Africa. 2011. 12th edition. Juta law & Co. LTD: Cape Town

Venter, Albert & Chris, Landsberg. 2011. *Government and Politics in South Africa.* 4th edition. Van Schaik Publishers: Pretoria

Part V: Metropolitan Councils

Introduction

When our Constitution came into effect in 1996, it provided a system of municipal authorities. These municipalities are divided into three categories, namely category A Municipality known as Metros, category B Municipality known as Local Municipality and category C Municipality known as District Municipality. This essay will focus on the category A Municipality.

1. Metropolitan Councils: Metros

The metros that are being established in the local spheres of government in South Africa are six, "namely Cape Town, Port Elizabeth (Nelson Mandela), Durban(eThekwini), Johannesburg, The East Rand (Ekurhuleni) and Pretoria (Tshwane)" (Venter and Landsberg, 2011:136). There are also two new metros namely, Buffalo City and Mangaung. And this brings the number to eight metros. A metropolitan municipality is a municipality which has an exclusive legislative and executive authority in its area of jurisdiction. These metros are sometimes called megacities or unicities. They are "the mother or parent city of a state, or a capital and also refers to any large city or complex of municipality authorities" (Venter and Landsberg, 2011:136).

These metropolitan councils have:

(a) High population density

(b) Intense movement of people, goods and services like the Bus Rapid Transport.

(c) Extensive public infrastructure in place like roads and education facilities

(d) Diverse economy like mining, manufacturing and tourism.

2. The differences between the Mayor and the Executive Mayor of a municipality

A Mayor is a person in charge of the council in a town or city and an Executive Mayor is a senior person with executive authority in the council or municipality. The Mayor focuses on ceremonial functions and the Executive mayor in executive functions. The Constitution of the Republic of South Africa does not provide any information or office of the Mayor or executive Mayor. These differences, powers and functions of the Mayor and the Executive Mayor can be found from the Municipality Structures Act 117 of 1998.

Functions and powers of a Mayor

We will start with the functions and powers of a Mayor as provided for by the Municipality Structures Act117 of 1998. It says "The mayor of a municipality presides at meetings of the executive committee and performs the duties including any ceremonial functions, and exercises the powers delegated to the mayor by the municipal council or the executive committee" (Government Gazette, 1998:23).

Functions and powers of the Executive Mayor

The following are some of the functions and powers of the Executive Mayor as stated in the Municipality Structures Act117 of 1998: "An executive mayor is entitled to receive reports from committees of the municipal council and to forward these reports together with a recommendation to the council when the matter cannot be disposed of by the executive mayor in terms of the executive mayors delegated powers. The executive mayor must identify the needs of the municipality: review and evaluate those needs in order of priority, recommend to the municipal council strategies, programmed and services to address priority needs through the integrated development plan, and the estimates of revenue and expenditure taking into account any applicable national and provincial development plans: and recommend or determine the best way including partnership and other approaches to deliver those strategies: programmes and services to the maximum benefit of the community. The executive mayor in performing the duties of office must identify evaluate progress against the key performance indicators; review the performance of the municipality in order to improve (i) the economy, efficiency and effectiveness of the municipality, (ii) the efficiency of credit control and revenue and debt collection services: And (iii) the implementation of the municipality's by-laws"(Government Gazette, 1998:24). We can conclude by saying the Mayor is more involved in ceremonial functions and the Executive mayor in executive functions.

3. Mayoral removal procedures from office

President Jacob Zuma cannot remove any elected Mayor of a municipality as he so wishes. It is only the Municipal Council that can remove a Mayor. The procedure to be followed when removing a Mayor is not provided in the Constitution but can be found in the Municipality Structures Act 117 of 1998. It says "A municipal council, by resolution may remove its executive mayor or deputy executive mayor from office. Prior notice of an intention to move a motion for the removal of the executive mayor or deputy executive mayor must be given" (Government Gazette, 1998:25).

Conclusion

Metropolitan Councils play an important role in providing goods and services in South Africa, improve infrastructure and grow our economy.

Bibliography

Venter, Albert & Chris, Landsberg. 2011. *Government and Politics in South Africa.* 4th edition. Van Schaik Publishers: Pretoria

Republic of South Africa Government Gazette, 1998. *Local Governmemnt: Municipality Structures Act no.117, 1998*, Vol.402, pp 23-24

About the author

Prophet Richard M. Mbokodo is the founder of Jesus is Lord Ministries, graduate from Phumelela Bible College with a Licentiate in Ministerial Theology, publisher-Mbokodo Publishers-and businessman, marriage officer and presently studying B Admin- Degree in Public Management-at the University of Pretoria, majoring in Administration, business management, financial accounting, economics, psychology, communication, academic information, political science, industrial psychology; and self-studying publishing part-time.

God has blessed him with 16 spiritual sons and daughters who are pastors serving the Lord. He had been in heaven 19 times (since 2007) and has seen Jesus our Lord and Saviour face to face. God gave him the grace to visit heaven every year during the month of May. He has seen angels, Peter, Abraham, the white throne of God and had been in paradise and had also seen the glimpse of hell. The Lord Jesus visited him on the 4th of January 2007. He has finished the Bible from Genesis to Revelation 23 times. God is using him mightily to change people's lives through the saving and healing power of our Lord Jesus Christ.